THE SAND LABYRINTH

MEDITATION AT YOUR FINGERTIPS

D1523959

THE SAND LABYRINTH

MEDITATION AT YOUR FINGERTIPS

Lauren Artress

JOURNEY EDITIONS
Boston • Tokyo • Singapore

First published in 2000 by Journey Editions, an imprint of Periplus Editions (HK) Ltd, with editorial offices at 153 Milk Street, Boston, Massachusetts 02109.

Library of Congress Cataloging-in-Publication Data
Artress, Lauren, 1945–
    The sand labyrinth : meditation at your fingertips / Lauren Artress.-- 1st ed.
        p. cm.
    ISBN 1-885203-99-3 (kt)
    1. Labyrinths--Religious aspects. 2. Meditation. 3. Spiritual life. I. Title.
BL325.L3 A78 2000
291.3'7--dc21   00-027046

Distributed by

NORTH AMERICA
Tuttle Publishing
Distribution Center
Airport Industrial Park
364 Innovation Drive
North Clarendon, VT
05759-9436
Tel: (802) 773-8930
Tel: (800) 526-2778
Fax: (802) 773-6993

JAPAN
Tuttle Publishing
RK Building, 2nd Floor
2-13-10 Shimo-Meguro,
Meguro-Ku
Tokyo 153 0064
Tel: (03) 5437-0171
Fax: (03) 5437-0755

ASIA PACIFIC
Berkeley Books Pte Ltd
5 Little Road #08-01
Singapore 536983
Tel: (65) 280-1330
Fax: (65) 280-6290

First edition
06 05 04 03 02 01 00   10 9 8 7 6 5 4 3 2 1

Box and cover design by Gopa Illustration and Design
Book design by Joyce Weston

Manufactured in China

CONTENTS

INTRODUCTION

Welcome to the Sand Labyrinth. This kit was created to make it possible for you to use the labyrinth in your office or home, or while away on retreat or vacation. You may have prior experience with labyrinths, or you may be learning about them for the first time. Either way, there are a few simple guidelines to know as you venture into the world of hand-traced labyrinths.

The labyrinth pattern is an archetypal form found all over the world. It dates back thousands of years. No one knows who created any of the labyrinth forms, but we do know from experience that embedded within each design is a pattern that somehow quiets our deep inner being so we can hear our own wisdom and the wisdom attempting to reach us. Whether walked or traced in sand, the labyrinth pattern is a powerful tool for reflection, meditation, realignment, and a deeper knowledge of the Self.

Chartres Cathedral, an hour south of Paris, houses what is perhaps the world's best-known labyrinth. The most elaborate of the labyrinth patterns, with eleven circuits, dates back to the

twelfth century. The classical seven-circuit—also known as the Cretan, Celtic, and Hopi medicine wheel—is the oldest known labyrinth, dating back four to five thousand years. It is round or sometimes kidney-shaped. Other labyrinth forms have been in such varying places as ancient Rome, the American Southwest, and Jewish mystical texts.

Labyrinths are not mazes, although in the English language the words *labyrinth* and *maze* are frequently confused. Mazes contain cul-de-sacs and dead ends. They have more than one entrance and more than one exit and are designed to make us lose our way; they're a game.

Labyrinths have the exact opposite purpose: they are

designed to help us find our way. They have only one path—
from the outer edge into the center and back out again.
Through the act of trusting the path, of giving up conscious
control of how things should go and being receptive to our
inner state, we can be opened up to a whole new world. It
seems that through the beautiful flow of their sacred patterns,
labyrinths help us ground ourselves.

Because there is only one path, the word "circuit" is used to
describe the number of times the path circles around the center. The classical seven-circuit labyrinth goes around seven
times; the eleven-circuit labyrinth meanders around the
center eleven times.

Many labyrinths, including the seven- and eleven-circuit ones, are "non-linear," meaning that the path goes through the four quadrants in a non-sequential way. One enters in the first quadrant, moves through the second, then back to the first, then to the third, and back to the second. As you move through a non-linear labyrinth, you lose your sense of where you are in the pattern and enter into a pleasurable state of timelessness. Some people find this type of surrender particularly relaxing and refreshing.

Labyrinths come in all sizes—from the forty-two-foot labyrinth at Chartres Cathedral to the twenty-four-inch one found in the wall outside La Lucca Cathedral in Lucca, Italy. At the Lucca labyrinth, one traces the pattern with one's finger in order to quiet the mind before entering the cathedral. At Veriditas, the World-Wide Labyrinth Project at Grace Cathedral, we have even heard about prison inmates who used toothpicks to trace the labyrinth found on our letterhead! So size does not matter as long as the integrity of the design is present.

Labyrinths were very popular during medieval times. As many as twenty-two of the eighty Gothic cathedrals housed labyrinths. In our present day we are experiencing a rediscovery of the labyrinth as a spiritual tool. Many communities are coming together to construct labyrinths in their community parks. Spiritual centers are creating them for those on retreat.

Hospitals are building permanent labyrinths for patients and staff. Cancer support groups use them for strength and finding one's way through difficult times. Patients at hypertension clinics walk them to reduce stress. The staff use them for taking a much needed time-out during a stress-filled day.

The eleven-circuit labyrinth is the one most widely replicated today. In the early 1990s, two such labyrinths were created at Grace Cathedral in San Francisco. Hundreds of thousands of visitors have walked these Cathedral labyrinths and the idea has proliferated from there. As of this writing, hundreds of eleven-circuit labyrinths are being created around the world.

For this Sand Labyrinth, we have chosen two patterns: the classical seven-circuit labyrinth and the eleven-circuit medieval labyrinth, both non-linear. By using sand to trace the labyrinth, we have added an important tactile element. Sand is a sensuous, easy-to-move material that will allow your natural flow to come forth. And the use of natural materials allows an energetic flow between the pattern and the person using it.

HOW TO USE THIS KIT

In your Sand Labyrinth box are this book, a bag of sand, two labyrinth patterns, and the wooden box. Begin by reading this section through and then choosing the labyrinth you want to begin with. Place it face up in the bottom of the wooden box with the entrance (the opening) at the bottom of the box, nearest your body. Insert the small placeholder pin at the opening of the labyrinth. (You probably will not need this pin after the first few times you use the Sand Labyrinth.) Open the bag of sand and measure out about one-half cup. (You might want to store the remaining sand in a pottery bowl or a nice jar that you can keep near your labyrinth.) Pour the sand evenly over the labyrinth pattern in the box. Use your hands to spread it evenly, or slowly shake the box until the sand is evenly spread. When you first use the Sand Labyrinth, you'll probably want to use less sand so that you can more easily see the path. As you become more familiar with meditating with the Sand Labyrinth, you may want to add more sand so you can proceed by touch alone.

Once you have smoothed the sand, find the opening and rest your finger in the sand. Begin tracing the pattern. You will want to keep your eyes open until you are familiar with the pattern. Be patient with yourself. If you get lost or "off the path," especially with the more complicated eleven-circuit labyrinth, simply smooth the sand and begin again. I know many people who found that labyrinth difficult at first. Don't be too goal-oriented about getting to the center or "doing it right." Simply let yourself pay attention to where you are on the path.

The Sand Labyrinth is designed for use any time you want

a time-out from your day. You may want to keep it in your office or home or take it with you on retreat when you have time to yourself. Keep it within easy reach. You can use it any time during the day, but it may be especially helpful at times of stress, decision making, or during a sleepless night. Use it as a meditation to quiet your mind or as a tool of insight to come to terms with a difficult situation.

Labyrinths are especially helpful during those difficult life transitions that activate our fears. The experience of walking or tracing the labyrinth pattern strengthens and sustains a calm center within us where we know that everything will be all right. When you're experiencing stress, you may want to trace the labyrinth just once before continuing your day, or take time out to trace it several times in succession.

People have different experiences each time they interact with a labyrinth, because each time they bring a different inner landscape to the experience. This is true even if you repeat the tracing several times in succession.

Over the years that I have worked with labyrinths I have also found that people experience different end-results with the different labyrinths. The classical seven-circuit labyrinth has fewer turns and therefore provides more of an open-road experience. It takes you through the path in long, broad sweeps as you wind your way to the center. People who walk it seem to come out in a relaxed, extroverted mind-set.

You might choose to use the classical seven-circuit labyrinth when you are preparing for an important meeting and want to be calm, extroverted, and on top of things in the presence of others. This labyrinth can also help you prepare to enter your day with an alert, relaxed attitude.

By contrast, the eleven-circuit labyrinth takes you to the center by a series of left turns and right turns that balances the hemispheres of the brain and the energy centers in the body. It offers a complex, challenging path and is a powerful tool for quieting the mind and receiving insight and guidance. It can take you deeply into yourself. Most people who use this labyrinth come out of it in a reflective, introverted state. You may want to follow up with some quiet time and perhaps journal about your experiences.

You may elect to use the eleven-circuit labyrinth when you have the time to retreat from the world or if you are working on a sinewy problem in your workplace that needs to be handled adeptly.

It may be helpful to think of the labyrinth meditation in three phases:

1. Going in, which provides a releasing, quieting, and an emptying experience.

2. Being in the center of the labyrinth to receive whatever there is to receive.
3. Following the same path back out to return to the world.

Some people think of these three stages as Releasing, Receiving, and Returning back to the everyday world.

Generally, on the way in, people experience a sense of shedding of everyday thoughts. This shedding leaves them open to receiving insights, guidance, or peace of mind, especially at the center, yet this can happen anytime throughout the experience. The time spent returning is helpful for reflection and integration of the experience.

These labyrinths can be used in an infinite number of ways. Besides quieting the mind and balancing your energies, they can bring you comfort and solace. If feelings of sadness, grief, or pain surface, allow yourself to release the feelings. The labyrinth provides an invisible process of movement, so when your experience is over—provided it is not rushed or cut short—any feelings that have surfaced will move toward resolution.

The labyrinth is particularly useful for confused or tangled feelings. The winding path seems to provide a place to reflect on the tugs and pulls you may be feeling but have been unable to identify. If you are using either of these labyrinths to address a specific situation in your life, such as a question weighing on your mind, it is important that you take as much time as you need to in order to quiet your mind. Then you can draw your attention gently to that which you would hope to focus on.

You cannot control or manipulate your labyrinth experiences, so it is not wise to take an "agenda" with you into the labyrinth. Rather, once your mind becomes quieter, you can gently bring your attention toward that which you hope to resolve or receive insight into. At first, you may find your attention flying all over the place. If that happens, just keep tracing the pattern until your mind settles down.

Because the labyrinth is a deep intuitive tool, it can provide a place where you can feel through a decision you are about to make or a problem with which you are confronted. If you bring a question of discernment into the labyrinth, avoid clear-cut "yes or no" thinking, allowing instead an open, receptive approach to whatever you are exploring or feeling through in the labyrinth.

Dreamwork is possible in the labyrinth as well. Simply allow your mind to become quieter and then gently bring to awareness whatever you remember of a dream. As you find your way through the path, allow your intuitive and imaginative parts to come forward to add other dimensions to the dream material.

Sometimes forgotten memories come back to us on the

labyrinth. If this happens, explore them historically, drawing out every element of information your five senses can give you. (Explorations like, How old am I in this memory? What am I wearing? What am I feeling? What am I hearing? etc.) A realization may surface in your awareness that healing needs to occur; you might initiate an imaginary dialogue with the person or people involved to move toward reconciliation.

Use everything that happens during a labyrinth experience as a metaphor for your life. The turns in the path may become the turns we have made in our life, or the center may become the center of ourselves that we are searching for as we walk through life. You may become pleasantly disoriented and lose your sense of time. You may hear guidance in one short succinct message. Or you may be "seized by a mantra"—a repeated phrase—that enters your consciousness, repeats itself over and over, and then leaves as quickly as it came.

It is important to "experience your experience" throughout the labyrinth tracing. This cuts through unhelpful expectations and brings you into the present moment. Sometimes you may feel that nothing is happening; just let yourself experience what "nothing" feels like.

In this book, you will find five sections:

1. Allowing Healing into Your Life
2. Creativity as a Spiritual Practice

3. Discovering Your Soul Assignment

4. Awakening Self-knowledge

5. Experiences on the Path

Each section contains material for reflection and highlights a specific use of the labyrinth. The section on Healing addresses the kind of psycho-spiritual healing that can come about through reflection, receiving guidance, self-forgiveness, release of anger, and forgiveness of others. Often we need to consciously invite healing into our lives, and we can begin that process by imagining what our lives would be like without the wound we are struggling with.

Creativity often unfolds when people begin to use the labyrinth in their lives. Many people do not realize that to live a creative life is to live a spiritual life and that to live a spiritual life is to live a creative, flowing life open to the Spirit. In the Creativity section, the quotations were chosen to help you enter this flow.

Soul Assignment addresses how the path unfolds for the many of us who are searching for or recommitting to our true work in the world. Work, in this sense, can be what we do for a paycheck and/or how we make a difference.

The next section, Self-knowledge, has many different aspects to it: self-discovery, self-awareness, etc. But the message at its core is that there is a deep place of wisdom within our self that we can have entry into when we use the labyrinth.

The final section, Experiences on the Path, is a sharing of others' experiences as they use the labyrinth. The labyrinth allows us to see our lives in a symbolic way. We begin to see a larger picture unfold for us. As a result, our lives take on new and bigger meanings.

Included in these sections are many quotations from the great sages and from those who have used the labyrinth as a spiritual tool. You can browse through these quotations for your own nourishment. Or use them to prepare for your labyrinth meditation. Or perhaps they will suggest a mantra to you. It's entirely up to you.

Labyrinth experiences are cumulative. Over time they increase in ease and clarity. We become strengthened in some way that is hard to articulate. The experiences may feel insignificant, but this may simply mean that you are not yet aware of what is realigning itself unconsciously. Keep a gentle eye out for changes, shifts, and events that configure themselves differently in your life once you begin to use this tool.

Once you familiarize yourself with the two labyrinths in this kit, let yourself tailor the way you use them to fit your individual needs. The suggestions I've given are simply intended to get you started in the use of these wonderful tools. There is no right or wrong way to use a labyrinth. Enjoy!

ALLOWING HEALING INTO YOUR LIFE

THERE ARE MANY KINDS OF HEALING. Though some of us are seeking physical healing—which may happen from time to time in the labyrinth—all of us are in need of psycho-spiritual healing. Our psyches carry bruises from the past. Some of us have been so deeply hurt we feel hopelessly fragmented. It is through a process of releasing the old hurts by forgiving ourselves and others that mercy and tenderness can enter our lives. This is sometimes difficult because forgiveness itself is a process, not an event, so it happens gradually over time.

If we ignore these past hurts, we hinder ourselves in the service of bringing light into the world. If we hang on to our injuries, it can create resentment, which does no one any good.

The labyrinth is a place for you to let go of the pain contained in the deep wounds of the past. Healing rarely occurs in the way we expect it to happen. Allow the winding path of the labyrinth to take you where it will in your interior world. Trust the path, feel the feelings, let them go when they are over. As the pain, anger, frustration, and resentment become energized, they will move out of your being like clouds moving through the sky on a stormy day. Their release frees up new capacities within us.

A friend is someone who knows the song in your heart and sings it back to you when you forget how it goes.

The AIDS Memorial Quilt

The significant problems we face cannot be solved at the same level of thinking we were at when we created them.

Albert Einstein

That which does not destroy me makes me stronger.

Friedrich Nietzsche

All revelation is the revelation of how to search, how to struggle. It is not the revelation of results.

Jacob Needleman

Healing is a creative act, calling for all the hard work and dedication needed for other forms of creativity.

Bernie Siegel, M.D.,
Love, Medicine and Miracles

Until you learn to name your ghosts and to baptize your hopes, you have not yet been born; you are still the creation of others.

Marie Cardinal,
Words to Say It

The kingdom of heaven is within you and whoever knows himself or herself will find it. And having found it, you will know yourselves that you are sons and daughters and heirs of the Almighty, and will know that you are in God and God is in you.

Luke, chapter 17

We're victims of a terrible theft, left with all of the suffering but with no transcendental context into which to put it…. we are not instructed that suffering is a door to wisdom, that grace often works through loss, and that these are direct opportunities to grasp our true nature.

Mark Matousek

Our task is to release the new spirit from the old stone, however painful that will be. Then and only then can we say, "I am alive. I will be free."

Marion Woodman

The labyrinth introduces us to the idea of a wide and gracious path. It redefines the journey… from a vertical perspective that goes from earth up to heaven, to a horizontal perspective in which we are all walking the path together. The vertical path has gotten mired down in perfectionist associations, whereas the horizontal path communicates that we are all in this together.

Lauren Artress,
from *Walking a Sacred Path*

Be patient toward all that is unsolved in your
heart and try to love the questions themselves....
Do not now seek the answers which cannot be
given you because you would not be able to live
them and the point is to live everything. Live the
questions now. Perhaps you will then gradually,
without noticing it, live along some distant day
into the answer.

Rainer Maria Rilke,
Letters to a Young Poet

There is no human act that cannot be hallowed
into a path to God.

Martin Buber

Just to be is a blessing.
Just to live is holy.

Rabbi Abraham Joshua Heschel

Growing spiritually can be like a rollercoaster ride. Take comfort in the knowledge that the way down is only preparation for the way up.

Rabbi Nachman of Breslov,
The Empty Chair

The labyrinth guides us through the troubles of our lives to the grand mysterious patterns that shape the web of creation. It leads us toward the Source and eventually guides us home.

Walking a Sacred Path

The body only appears to be an enclosure. It is actually a passageway—like an entry to a cave or a cathedral. It is quite the opposite of the way we've been taught to perceive it.

Stephen R. Schwartz,
The Prayer of the Body

CREATIVITY AS
A SPIRITUAL PRACTICE

FINDING THE FLOW OF YOUR CREATIVE PROCESS is a spiritual path. And this path reveals itself as we align with the organic unfolding in our daily lives. You can find your own rhythm of unfolding as you trace the labyrinth.

Through responding to our unique pulsation, our own original rhythm, we find we are able to come into the present moment. It is as if we are looking into a creek that contains clear and flowing water. As we look into the water, we see life around us reflected back to us. If we hold those images as part of us, they begin to take on unexpected but welcome shapes and forms, piecing together a new reality.

The labyrinth is a place where we can enter our own natural flow. It can take us down a stream of associations that are uniquely our own and help us identify what it is within us that longs to be put into form in the outer world. It may be a vision for a new program for kids at risk, it may be a section of a book, or it may be a sense of spaciousness inside that allows an act of kindness toward a stranger.

Do not hurry, nor dally. Just allow yourself to open to your own interior rhythms, to enter your flow and find the unique and original pulsation that calls you to be truly yourself. There you will find wisdom.

The creative process is a spiritual path. This
adventure is about us, about the deep self, the
composer in all of us, about originality, meaning,
not that which is all new, but that which is fully
and originally ourselves.

Stephen Nachmanovitch,
Free Play

We have to realize that a creative being lives
within ourselves, whether we like it or not, and
that we must get out of its way, for it will not give
us peace until we do.

M. C. Richards,
Centering

If we fail to nourish our souls, they wither. Life becomes boring; it has not dimension. Without soul, we have no ears to hear great music, no perception to understand poetry or dreams, no eyes to appreciate fine art. The creative process shrivels in the absence of continual dialogue with soul. And creativity is what makes life worth living.

Marion Woodman

We re-activate soul when we see every moment, every meeting in life, every dream, every action as poetry and myth.

Robert Avens,
Imagination Is Reality

All the most important aspects of thought come from that which is thinking through us. And this process is the myth, one of the most profound things of life; it is creation itself, which becomes accessible and, in part, emerges and gives, of its own accord, a sense of direction to the human creature. It is something with which—if we use our brains and imagination—we are in partnership.

Sir Laurens van der Post

If you have dreamed it, it is already within you.

Kathleen Henry

The more faithfully you listen to the voice within you, the better you will hear what is sounding outside. And only she who listens can speak. Is this the starting point of the road towards the union of your two dreams—to be allowed in clarity of mind to mirror life and in purity of heart to mold it?

Dag Hammarskjold,
Markings

There are no days in life so memorable as those which vibrated to some stroke of the imagination.

Ralph Waldo Emerson

Think of a poem or a piece of music that you read or hear over and over again… each time you hear it a bit differently. You see it from images within yourself. You not only hear it differently, but it causes you to hear other things differently. The poetic image creates perceptions, modalities of perceiving…. It is drawing you into its landscapes and adding not only to your experiences but to your ways of experiencing.

Mary Watkins

When I examine my methods of thought…
I come to the conclusion that I owe more to the power of my imagination than to my ability to manipulate numbers.

Albert Einstein

God is not static. God is in constant creation,
constantly being created. We are not static, either.
We are in constant creation.

Cil Braun

You need chaos in your soul to give birth to a
dancing star.

Friedrich Nietzsche

A new human is being called forth to be a
creative participant in the further evolution of life
here on planet Earth.

L. Robert Keck,
Sacred Eyes

Perception is a mirror, not a fact. And what I look
on is my state of mind, reflected outward.

F. Vaughan and R. Walsh (eds.),
Accept this Gift

[The imagination frees] the mind-forged manacles of reason's tyranny.

William Blake,
The Marriage of Heaven and Hell

The importance of the labyrinth [is that] no matter where we are on our life's journey, no matter what tradition sparks the creative imagination, we may glimpse the divine.

Walking a Sacred Path

If the doors of perception were cleansed everything would appear to humans as it is: infinite. For (humans) have closed themselves up, till they see all things through narrow chinks in their caverns.

William Blake,
The Marriage of Heaven and Hell

The creative person seems to have a special talent for dipping into his intuitive, image-filled right hemisphere while harnessing the illuminating experience with his left brain.

Steven Zinker

So many people don't know how to inspire themselves. Use everything that moves you: music, walking by water, flowers, photographs of the enlightened ones. Inspiration helps so deeply in overcoming laziness, summons what the Sufis call "the fragrance of the Beloved" into everything.

Andrew Harvey,
Dialogues With A Modern Mystic

The purpose of craft is not so much to make beautiful things as it is to become beautiful inside while you are making those things.

Susan Gordon Lydon,
The Knitting Sutra

Upon entering the labyrinth, we sense that it is a symbol representing the whole. Our world of splits and divisions disappears for a few contented minutes. The seeker enters a nondualistic world, where clear thinking through the channel of intuition has a chance to emerge from deep within.

Walking a Sacred Path

Everything the Power of the World does is done in a circle.

Black Elk,
Black Elk Speaks

The woods would be very silent if no birds sang except the best.

Yiddish proverb

There must always be two kinds of art, escape art,
for one needs escape as he or she needs food and
deep sleep, and parable art, the art which shall
teach us to unlearn hatred and learn love.

W. H. Auden

The labyrinth does not engage our thinking
minds. It invites our intuitive, pattern-seeking,
symbolic mind to come forth.

Walking a Sacred Path

DISCOVERING YOUR SOUL ASSIGNMENT

"EVERY HUMAN BEING COMES TO EARTH with sealed orders," said Søren Kierkegaard. Many of us know the deep intuitive truth behind this statement and are looking for our "sealed orders."

When we search for our sealed orders, many of us feel that we are on an aimless road to nowhere rather than a spiritual path. Searching for our sealed orders is very much like being on a treasure hunt—a game many of us played as children. You cannot move further in the hunt without the next clue. You must find the clue and then follow it through until it leads to the next clue. This is true in the search for our sealed orders as well. You must pay attention to what is before you to find the clue. Our imaginations must be open so the clue speaks to us. Once we find the clue, we need to crack open the hidden meaning in order to harvest the wisdom contained within. And so each step of the way is discovered. Joseph Campbell's famous quote "Follow your bliss" is not bad advice, for within that bliss is a clue.

It is interesting to note that the word "clue" came directly from the labyrinth, for originally the turns were called "clews." So, if you don't have a clue as to where you are going, the labyrinth can offer you many "clews" and bring your path into focus. It can open your imagination—if you allow it—so you begin to see your world in a symbolic way.

Every[one]'s life is a fairytale, written by the finger of God.

Hans Christian Andersen

If the world is to be healed through human efforts, I am convinced it will be by ordinary people, people whose love for this life is even greater than their fear. People who can open to the web of life that called us into being and who can rest in the vitality of that larger body.

Joanna Macy

The soul may be the part of you that sees the dream.

Author unknown

We only die when we fail to take root in others.

Leon Trotsky

Loyalty to a petrified opinion never yet broke a chain or freed a human soul.

Mark Twain

Now there are varieties of gifts, but the same Spirit; and there are varieties of service, but the same Lord: and there are varieties of working, but it is the same God who inspires them all in every one. To each is given the manifestation of the Spirit for the common good. To one is given through the Spirit the utterance of wisdom, and to another the utterance of knowledge according to the same Spirit, to another faith by the same Spirit, to another the ability to distinguish between spirits, to another various kinds of tongues, to another the interpretation of tongues. All these are inspired by one and the same Spirit, who apportions to each one individually as he wills.

1 Corinthians 12:4–13

The labyrinth experience… helps us distinguish superficial extraneous thoughts from the "thoughts" that come from our soul level and that each of us longs to hear.

Walking a Sacred Path

And the day came when the risk to remain tight in a bud was more painful than the risk it took to blossom.

Anaïs Nin

There is a meaning in every journey that is unknown to the traveler.

Dietrich Bonhoeffer

Manifesting a vision is not static and definitely not linear; rather, it is an organic process of adapting and changing as we interact with many unknowns. A seed planted in the ground automatically adjusts as it interacts with rocks, roots, poor growing conditions, infertile soil, and so on. This is the way of growth and manifestation.

Gail Straub/David Gershon

The winding path of the labyrinth offers a blueprint for the psyche to meet the soul.

Walking a Sacred Path

What in your life is calling you?
When all the noise is silenced,
the meetings adjourned,
the lists laid aside,
and the wild iris blooms by itself in the dark
    forest,
what still pulls on your soul?

In the silence between your heartbeats
    hides a summons.
Do you hear it?
Name it, if you must,
or leave it forever nameless,
but why pretend it is not there?

Terma Collective, "The Box"
from *Remembering the Way*

There is a Light in this world, a Healing Spirit
more powerful than any darkness we may
encounter. We sometimes lose sight of this force
when there is suffering or too much pain. Then
suddenly the Spirit will emerge through the lives
of ordinary people who hear a call and answer in
extraordinary ways.

Mother Teresa

I live my life in growing orbits
which move out over the things of the world.
I am circling around God, around the ancient tower,
and I have been circling for a thousand years,
And I still don't know if I'm a falcon,
or a storm,
or a great song.

Rainer Maria Rilke,
Selected Poems

Meditation is a new kind of thinking, a way of
leaving behind the physical brain, which can only
reflect the material world in its outer aspect. . . .
Meditation is the intensification of intelligence,
the warmth and light within things. Picture-
making or imaging unfolds from the action of
meditation. Images are reflections of the warmth
of meditation, they are a reflective intelligence.

Robert Sardello

The new temple of initiation is the world itself.

Robert Sardello

We ordinary people must forge our own beauty.
We must set fire to the greyness of our labor with
the art of our own lives.

Kenji Miyazawa

When you come to the edge of all that you know,
you must believe one of two things: there will be
earth to stand on, or you will be given the wings
to fly.

Author unknown

Experiencing the silence within is like opening a
hidden door to the soul. It takes enormous patience.

Walking a Sacred Path

AWAKENING
SELF-KNOWLEDGE

CONTAINED WITHIN ALL THE MYSTICAL TRADITIONS of the world is one mystery rarely understood in the noisy, neon consciousness of the Western world: If you know yourself in the innermost chambers of your being, there you can also come to know Divine Presence.

If we know ourselves only superficially, we live in a prison made with bars shaped from our own denial of who we truly are, our lack of truth-telling, and our inability to see ourselves and others in a compassionate way. We block the light that has the potential to come through us. Instead we let our energies be directed into maintaining the status quo and no spiritual maturation occurs. I often ask people: What is the difference between a mature fifty-year-old person and an immature fifty-year-old? It's the ability to reflect and learn from difficult experiences.

The labyrinth is a place where you can begin to come to terms with yourself. There you can open to the mystery within you and begin to sense an unfolding path to forgiveness, gentleness, and wisdom.

It is life itself that must be our practice. It is not enough to hear spiritual truth or even to have our own spiritual insights. Every aspect of what happens to us must become part of a learning experience.

Diane Mariechild

At the center of a great tornado is a point of peace. Thus does the story go. It can be found. And thus it is with all the storms of life. They lead to peace if you are not a leaf.

Alice Bailey

No one can know God that has not first known himself. Go to the depths of the soul, the secret place… to the roots, and to the heights; for all that God can do is focused there.

Meister Eckhart

Every blade of grass has its Angel that bends over
it and whispers, "grow, grow."

The Talmud

The enemy of whole vision is reasoning power's
divorce from the imagination.

William Blake

We so often see ourselves as failing, but God sees
us as only rising, and methinks God has the
greater insight.

Julian of Norwich,
Showings

I have only three enemies. My favorite enemy, the
one most easily influenced for the better, is the
British Empire. My second enemy, the Indian
people, is far more difficult. But my most formidable
opponent is a man named Mohandas K. Gandhi.
With him I seem to have very little influence.

Mohandas K. Gandhi,
known as "Mahatma"

Our deepest fear is not that we are inadequate. Our deepest fear is that we are powerful beyond measure. It is our Light, not our darkness, that most frightens us. We ask ourselves, who am I to be brilliant, gorgeous, talented, fabulous? Actually, who are you NOT to be? You are a child of God. Your playing small does not serve the world.

There is nothing enlightened about shrinking so that other people won't feel insecure around you. We were born to manifest the glory of God that is within us. It is not just in some of us; it is in everyone. And as we let our own Light shine, we unconsciously give other people permission to do the same. As we are liberated from our own fear, our presence automatically liberates others.

Marianne Williamson,
Return to Love

The real voyage of discovery consists not in seeking new landscapes but in having new eyes.

Marcel Proust

The will of God will not lead you where the grace of God cannot go.

Author unknown

Truth is knowing that we know we lie.

W. H. Auden

The reasonable man adapts himself to the world, the unreasonable one persists in trying to adapt the world to himself. Therefore all progress depends on the unreasonable man.

George Bernard Shaw

The average man, who does not know what to do with his life, wants another one which will last forever.

Anatole France

The future ain't what it used to be.

Arthur C. Clarke

You gain strength, courage and confidence by every experience in which you really stop to look fear in the face. You are able to say to yourself, "I lived through this horror. I can take the next thing that comes along." You must do the thing you think you cannot do.

Eleanor Roosevelt,
You Learn by Living

People are divided into three groups:
   Those that make things happen
   Those who watch things happen
   Those who ask "What happened?"
Which one applies to you?

Forbes Magazine

I've been trying for some time to develop a lifestyle that doesn't require my presence.

Garry Trudeau

You must have a room or a certain hour of the day or so, where you do not know who your friends are, you don't know what you owe anybody or what they owe you—but a place where you can simply experience and bring forth what you are and what you might be.... At first, you may find nothing's happening... but if you have a sacred place and use it, take advantage of it, something will happen.

Joseph Campbell

The archetype for the self and the archetype for God are indistinguishable.

Carl Jung

One might even be born a blind leper in a ring of fire and if your mind is focused only on the truth of the vastness of being you will always be in heaven.

Stephen Levine

To be pilgrims walking on a path to the next century, we need to participate in the dance between silence and image, ear and eye, inner and outer. We need to change our seeking into discovery, our drifting into pilgrimage.

Walking a Sacred Path

In a world of fugitives, those taking the opposite direction will always be said to be running away.

T. S. Eliot

We are light going through a prism. The light is always there, and we can act as its prism, concentrate and filter it. We make of the light of the cosmos, a rainbow with a mouth and arms.

Jarret Smith

You are the veil that hides the paradise you seek.

Saint Brendan

One does not become enlightened by imagining figures of light, but by making the darkness conscious.

Carl Jung

If you bring forth what is within you, it will save you; if you do not bring forth what is within you, it will destroy you.

The Gospel of Thomas

It takes an honest person to know when to break the rules.

Author unknown

The archetype that is enlivened in the labyrinth is the archetype of transformation. The circle, which expresses wholeness and unity, is the central archetype, which Jung called the Self.

Walking a Sacred Path

EXPERIENCES ON THE PATH

A S WE START TO MOVE THROUGH THE LABYRINTH and come into the present moment, we can begin to see our lives in a larger context. All the pressure is off and we can surrender to the path, discover a deeper capacity of breathing, and come into our own unique rhythm.

The reason that so many of us feel lost and are searching is that we judge what we do experience through filters of which we are rarely even aware, such as: "What will people think?" or "My experience isn't as profound as hers." These kinds of thoughts stop us from valuing our own experience. It is so important, as we walk our life's path, that we learn to trust our own experiences, not discount them or invalidate them because they do not compare to other people's experiences.

Truth be told, no one of us knows where we are going in life. We feel vulnerable to the unexpected turns that occur—such as a sudden death or loss of a job—that are out of our immediate control. To experience our path is to acknowledge the possibility that "something greater" is attempting to live itself out through our lives. On the labyrinth, as in our lives, we must simply learn to value our own presence. The feeling of not knowing where we are going can challenge our need for control and order in our lives. Sometimes our linear minds become so confounded that we want to give up the exercise of moving through the labyrinth.

But as we continue to move through the labyrinth, we begin to realize that there is mystery to life. There is a hidden process behind the everyday external world that we do not notice when we are attached to the flat-bottomed reality that we move about in everyday. Valuing our experience, just as it is, is a key to opening to the Mystery held within everyday life.

The quotes in this section capture some of the discoveries made by labyrinth walkers. Imagine what discoveries can be yours as you trace the labyrinth in the sand.

Traveler, there is no path. Paths are made by walking.

Pablo Neruda

Many people pray and receive the answer to their prayers, but ignore them—or deny them, because the answers didn't come in the expected form.

Sophy Burnham

I thought of a labyrinth of labyrinths, of one sinuous spreading labyrinth that would encompass the past and the future and in some way involve the stars.

Jorge Luis Borges,
The Garden of Forking Paths

When you're learning to face the path at your pace, every choice is worth your while.

Indigo Girls

Divinity is like a wheel, a circle, a whole.

Hildegard von Bingen

My Lord God

I have no idea of where I am going.

I do not see the road ahead of me.

I cannot know for certain where it will end.

Nor do I really know myself, and the fact that I
    think I am following your will does not mean
    that I actually am doing so.

But I believe that the desire to please you does in
    fact please you, and I hope I have that desire in
    all that I am doing.

I hope that I will never do anything apart from
    that desire.

And I know that if I do this you will lead me by the
    right road, though I may know nothing about it.

Therefore I will trust you always though I may
    seem to be lost and in the shadow of death, I
    will not fear for you are with me and you will
    never leave me, to face my perils alone.

Amen.

                                    Thomas Merton

The completed journey always ends with a
return, a homecoming to the ordinary world
of conventional reality that was left behind.
This world has been transformed, if our journey
has been successful, into a new world, seen with
fresh eyes. The end of the journey is the
beginning of a new, empowered way of life.

Ralph Metzner,
Opening to Inner Light

When I [entered the labyrinth] it felt like going
through a birth canal, like being born into my
own life.

Dawn J. Jipthrott

The labyrinth made me realize that although we
will, and *must*, take turns in life, it all leads in one
direction.

Vera Faulhaber

First, it is a process of surrender. The path is set, you simply follow it. This in itself is a new experience for many people—a unique combination of activity and passivity. Secondly, the path is not predictable, and thereby short-circuits that lobe so dominant in many of our brains that strives constantly to know the future. And since the future is, in truth, unknowable, walking the labyrinth relieves us of that exhausting struggle.

[The labyrinth] is a sign of the body at prayer, a liturgical dance, of a people dancing the holy path together.

Cynthia Winton-Henry

Walking the labyrinth, I came to see the universal
pattern that lay within me, within life itself—the
labyrinth being a metaphor for life. Always
turning, facing new directions, yet I was never
completely able to stray from the path.…
Meandering and twisting to and fro, no one can
be sure exactly where they are in the labyrinth,
how far from the center, how far from the end;
just as in life, only one thing is certain: You go out
exactly the same way you came in.

Michelle Naomi Baer

On one walk you may discover that the most
direct way from one place to another is rarely a
straight line. On another you may find standing at
the center of the labyrinth to be standing at the
center of Earth itself. On yet another you may
exit saying, "Everywhere the center, everywhere
the edge." The possibilities are inexhaustible.

Harvey Manchester

I believe that my work with the labyrinth has enabled me to mature spiritually in ways that would not have ordinarily been possible. When I am facing a difficult time in life I take that issue into the labyrinth with me. When I am feeling blessed and grateful, I take those feelings with me into the labyrinth. When friends or family need prayers, I pray for them in the labyrinth. The labyrinth has become a guide for me in just about every area of my life—because every time I walk it, my mind quiets, my heart opens and I can hear God's voice.

Aimee Dominique

Life is walking a labyrinth. I cannot always know which way I will turn, or even see far ahead, but there are no tricks. It is not a maze, no chance of getting lost, trust in the path that has been laid for me or in the path that I have chosen. Walk it in trust, stop when a break is necessary, and know that the center is always there.

Elizabeth H. Wiggins

The gift of the labyrinth to me is that at every
bend in the road, instead of getting worried about
what comes next, I can stop or slow down and
look where I've been and where I'm going.

Judith Boel

The labyrinth can make it easier for most of us if
we surrender to the experience: allowing not
forcing, receiving not shaping, accepting not
judging. We must be like the martial artist whose
power comes not from making things happen but
from surrendering to what occurs and then
responding from a centered place.

Walking a Sacred Path

Most of the experiences that occur in the
labyrinth are unexpected. They are guided
by a sacred wisdom, a creative intelligence that
knows more about what we need than do our
conscious selves.

Walking a Sacred Path

Until one is committed, there is hesitancy, the chance to draw back, always ineffectiveness. Concerning all acts of initiative (and Creation) there is one elementary truth, the ignorance of which kills countless ideas and splendid plans.

I have learned a deep respect for one of Goethe's couplets:

Whatever you can do, or dream you can, begin it.
Boldness has genius, power and magic in it.

W. H. Murray,
The Scottish Himalayan Expedition

The moment one definitely commits oneself then Providence moves too. All sorts of things occur to help that would never otherwise have occurred. A whole stream of events issues from the decision, raising in one's favor all manner of unforeseen incidents, meetings, and material assistance, which no man would have dreamed would come his way.

Johann Wolfgang Von Goethe